D1716340

BIGFOOT

BY RAY McCLELLAN

EPIC

BELLWETHER MEDIA • MINNEAPOLIS, MN

EPIC BOOKS are no ordinary books. They burst with intense action, high-speed heroics, and shadows of the unknown. Are you ready for an Epic adventure?

This edition first published in 2014 by Bellwether Media, Inc.

No part of this publication may be reproduced in whole or in part without written permission of the publisher. For information regarding permission, write to Bellwether Media, Inc., Attention: Permissions Department, 5357 Penn Avenue South, Minneapolis, MN 55419.

Library of Congress Cataloging-in-Publication Data

McClellan, Ray.
 Bigfoot / by Ray McClellan.
    pages cm. – (Epic. Unexplained Mysteries)
 Summary: "Engaging images accompany information about Bigfoot. The combination of high-interest subject matter and light text is intended for students in grades 2 through 7"– Provided by publisher.
 Audience: Ages 7-12.
 Includes bibliographical references and index.
 ISBN 978-1-62617-103-9 (hardcover : alk. paper)
 1. Sasquatch–Juvenile literature. 2. Yeti–Juvenile literature. I. Title.
 QL89.2.S2M3655 2014
 001.944–dc23

                              2013035888

TABLE OF CONTENTS

COULD IT BE BIGFOOT?

A hiker walks deep into the woods. He is looking for the famous Bigfoot. Suddenly, he hears a loud shriek from behind a nearby tree.

A dark shape rushes through the woods. The hiker grabs his camera and snaps a photo. The picture shows what looks like a hairy arm. Was it Bigfoot?

7

WHAT IS BIGFOOT?

People around the world report seeing a strange creature in the woods. They describe it as half human and half gorilla. They call the hairy beast Bigfoot.

USE YOUR WORDS

People say Bigfoot communicates with howls and grunts. He might also knock on trees.

CANADA

UNITED STATES

N
W E
S

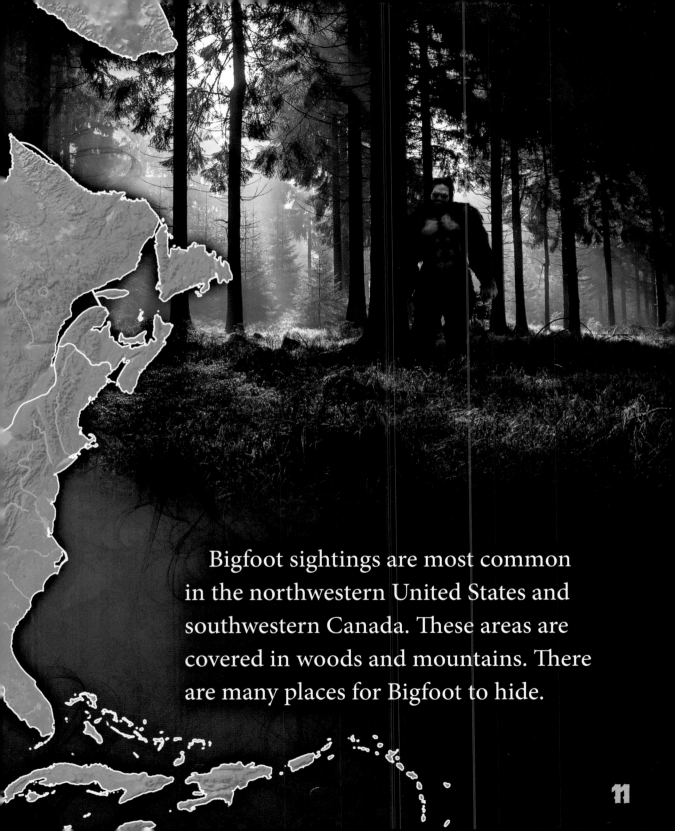

Bigfoot sightings are most common in the northwestern United States and southwestern Canada. These areas are covered in woods and mountains. There are many places for Bigfoot to hide.

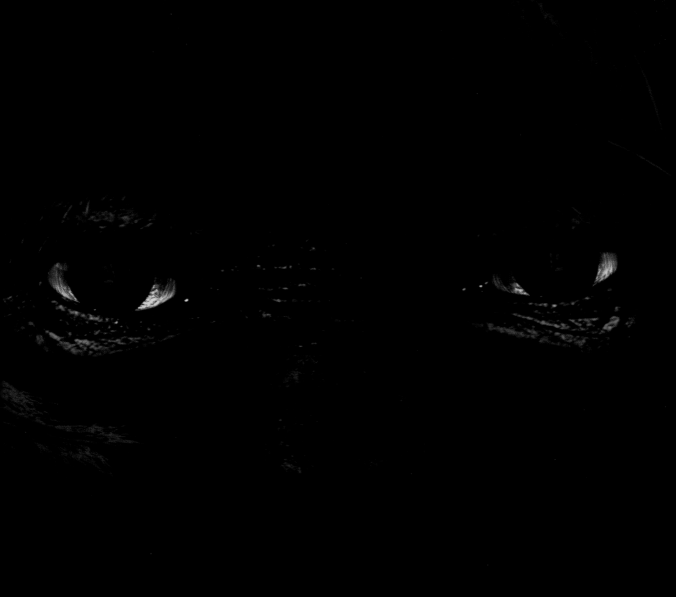

Bigfoot is believed to be a **nocturnal** creature. People think it waits until night to hunt or **forage** for food. Many reports describe huge eyes glowing in the dark.

WHAT'S THAT SMELL?

People who have come close to Bigfoot say that the creature smells like swamps, rotting food, or skunks.

FACT OR FICTION?

Many **theories** try to explain what Bigfoot is. Some people think it is a *Gigantopithecus*. This **extinct** animal walked the earth millions of years ago.

STANDING TALL

Gigantopithecus means "giant ape." Adult males stood up to 10 feet (3 meters) tall!

GIGANTOPITHECUS

HUMAN

15

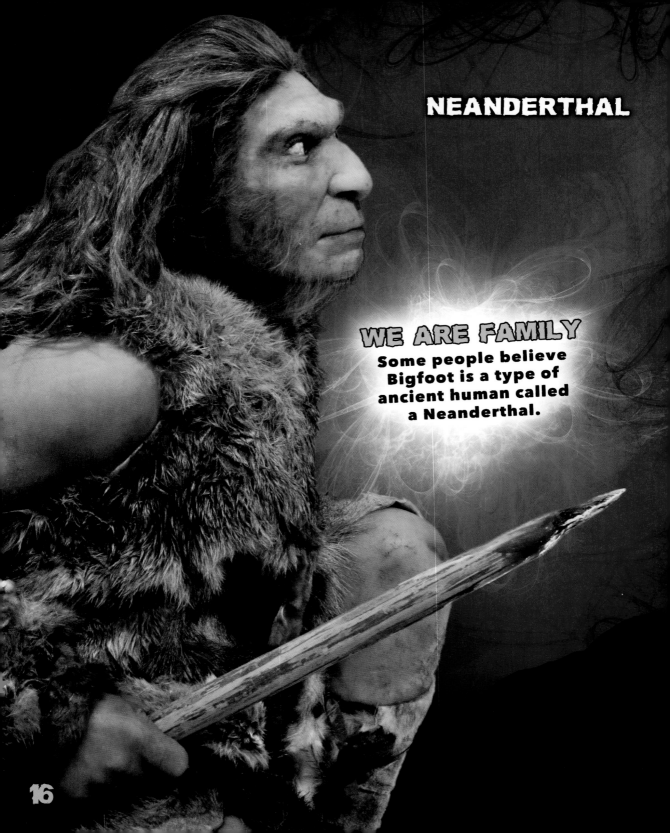

NEANDERTHAL

WE ARE FAMILY

Some people believe Bigfoot is a type of ancient human called a Neanderthal.

Others argue that Bigfoot is a wild human. They think a man left the city to live in the wilderness. They believe he adapted to life in

Skeptics believe that Bigfoot is a myth. They say that people are seeing large bears. Some sightings have been proven to be hoaxes.

Many people have snapped photos of strange shapes in the woods. But so far no pictures have proven that Bigfoot is real. Does Bigfoot roam the woods or our imaginations?

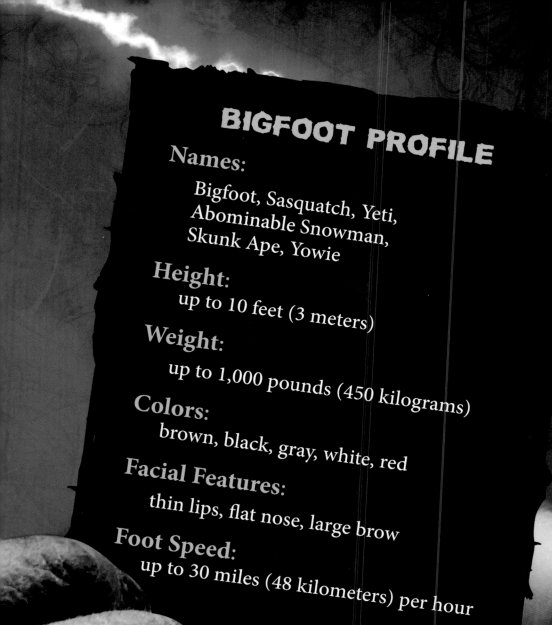

BIGFOOT PROFILE

Names:

Bigfoot, Sasquatch, Yeti,
Abominable Snowman,
Skunk Ape, Yowie

Height:
up to 10 feet (3 meters)

Weight:

up to 1,000 pounds (450 kilograms)

Colors:
brown, black, gray, white, red

Facial Features:
thin lips, flat nose, large brow

Foot Speed:
up to 30 miles (48 kilometers) per hour

GLOSSARY

adapted—changed to survive in a new place

extinct—no longer living

forage—to search a large area for food

hoaxes—attempts to trick people into believing something

myth—an untrue story that many people believe

nocturnal—most active at night

skeptics—people who doubt the truth of something

theories—ideas that explain something

wilderness—undeveloped land that is home to plants and animals

TO LEARN MORE

At the Library

Burgan, Michael. *The Unsolved Mystery of Bigfoot*. North Mankato, Minn.: Capstone Press, 2013.

Hawkins, John. *Bigfoot and Other Monsters*. New York, N.Y.: PowerKids Press, 2012.

Troupe, Thomas Kingsley. *The Legend of Bigfoot*. Mankato, Minn.: Picture Window Books, 2011.

On the Web

Learning more about Bigfoot is as easy as 1, 2, 3.

1. Go to www.factsurfer.com.

2. Enter "Bigfoot" into the search box.

3. Click the "Surf" button and you will see a list of related Web sites.

With factsurfer.com, finding more information is just a click away.

INDEX

The images in this book are reproduced through the courtesy of: Andreas Meyer, front cover (composite), p. 8 (composite); Mike Cherim, p. 4; Piotr Krzeslak, pp. 4-5; Anton Balazh, pp. 6-7 (composite); Uwe Zucchi/ EPA/ Newscom, p. 9; AridOcean, pp. 10-11; Greglith/ Val Thoermer, p. 11 (composite); Juan Martinez, pp. 12-13; Daderot/ Wikipedia, p. 15; Ulrich Perrey Deutsch Presse Agentur/ Newscom, p. 16; jordache/ Andreas Meyer, p. 17 (composite); Rinus Baak, p. 18; Tannis Toohey/ Getty Images, pp. 18-19; AFP/ Getty Images/ Newscom, p. 20 (top); Animals Animals/ SuperStock, p. 20 (bottom).